CONTENTS

The blue in the Mongolian flag represents the sky.
The red stripes initially represented Mongolia's socialist
beliefs, but a modern interpretation means liberty and
progress. The *soyombo* symbol is a national emblem.

Sukhbaatar Square, in the capital city Ulaanbaatar.

Mongolia is a large country located in Central Asia. It shares a border with Russia in the north and China in the south, and much of Mongolia's history is linked with these two nations. For many years, however, the land that is now Mongolia was the heart of a great empire in its own right, under the leadership of the thirteenth-century Mongol warlord Genghis Khan. Mongolia was a socialist state for much of the twentieth century, but with the collapse of Communism across Europe and the disintegration of the Soviet Union, Mongolia began its own move towards democracy.

Mongolia's border stretches for 8,225km and it is the nineteenth largest country in the world. However, it also is the least densely populated, with only 1.7 people per square kilometre. The area is divided into 21 administrative provinces, plus the capital city, Ulaanbaatar. These provinces are known as aimags.

Mongolia is a country of great natural beauty, with mountains, plateaus, lakes and desert regions. Large parts of the country are covered by prairie and steppe (dry, treeless areas covered in grass). The Gobi Desert lies in southern Mongolia and stretches for 1,300,000 sq km across Mongolia and China. The three main mountain regions lie in the north and west. The highest point is Huyten Peak, in the Altai Mountains, at 4,374m. The lowest point is Lake Hoh Nuur, at 518m above sea level.

Mongolia is completely landlocked. Because of this, and the barrier created by the Hangayn

MONGOLIA

MUNKHTUYA BOLD

Evans

TITLES IN THE COUNTRIES OF THE WORLD SERIES:

ARGENTINA · AUSTRALIA · BRAZIL · CANADA · CHILE · CHINA · EGYPT · FRANCE · GERMANY · INDIA · INDONESIA · ITALY · JAPAN · KENYA · MEXICO · NIGERIA · POLAND · RUSSIA · SOUTH KOREA · SPAIN · SWEDEN · UNITED KINGDOM · USA · VIETNAM

Published by Evans Brothers Limited
2A Portman Mansions
Chiltern Street
London W1U 6NR

Produced in association with Nepko, Mongolia

First published 2008

British Library Cataloguing in Publication Data
Bold, Munkhtuya
  Mongolia. - (Countries of the world)
  1. Mongolia - Juvenile literature
  I. Title
  915.1'7
  ISBN 978-99929-900-8-2

Translator: Badamdash D. Marhy
Editor: Sonya Newland
Designer: Nepko Publishing LLC
Picture researcher: L. Dorjbat

Series concept and design by
Monkey Puzzle Media Limited

Picture acknowledgements:
All photographs taken by Gamma agency (S. Tsatsralt) and Prophoto agency (J. Batbaatar) apart from 37t, which was kindly provided by V. Tsend-Ayush.

Endpapers (front): Night view of Ulaanbaatar city.
Title page: Mongolian guards at the Sukhbaatar square in Ulaanbaatar.
Imprint and contents pages: Blue sky in countryside.
Endpapers (back): Performing *Atga Noj* drama at the Drama Theatre.

Mountains, running from the northwest to the southeast, Mongolia does not enjoy a warm ocean climate, but has a more severe continental climate, characterised by long, cold winters and hot summers.

Many rare plants and animals have learned to survive in the extreme climatic conditions of Mongolia. Wolves, *mazalai* (desert bears), marmots, lynx, *argal* (wild mountain sheep), ibex, brown bears, beavers, sables, eagles, vultures, falcons, moose and deer are all found in different regions of the country.

ECONOMIC ACTIVITY

Mongolia is predominantly agricultural, and raising livestock is a particularly important economic activity. After the Second World War there was a rise in industries such as textiles and mining. Industry accounts for almost a quarter of Mongolia's GDP, even though it employs only around 10 per cent of the labour force. The country is rich in mineral resources such as gold, copper, iron, silver and crude oil, so mining is particularly important. Since 1921, when Mongolia gained independence, it has been developing international relations and large investments have been made in mining by investors from countries such as the USA, Canada, China, Russia and Italy.

KEY DATA

Official Name:	Mongolia
Area:	1,564,160 sq km
Population:	2,609,000 (2007 est.)
Official Language:	Mongolian
Main Cities:	Ulaanbaatar (capital), Erdenet, Darkhan, Selenge
GDP Per Capita:	US$2,100 (2006 est.)
Currency:	Tugrug (MNT)
Exchange Rate:	US$1 = 1,165 MNT £1 = 2,287.8 MNT

Sources: www.cia.gov
www.banjig.net

RELIGION

Around 50 per cent of the population of Mongolia is Buddhist. Around 40 per cent claim to follow no religion, and there are small groups of Muslims and Christians. At the start of the twentieth century, there were around 100,000 lamas (Buddhist monks) in Mongolia, roughly 30 per cent of the population at that time. However, between the 1920s and the 1940s the religion was suppressed and the monks were driven out or killed.

The volcano Uran Togoo, in Bulgan aimag.

The 800th anniversary of the Mongolian state, established by Genghis Khan (left).

PEOPLE

Mongolia has a population of just over 2.6 million. Almost 95 per cent of these are native Mongols. The rest are Turkic-speaking peoples (mainly Kazakhs), with some Chinese and Russians. The main population centre is the capital city, Ulaanbaatar, where more than one million people live.

During the socialist era there was a big drive to improve literacy in Mongolia and now nearly 98 per cent of the population can read and write. Forty per cent of Mongolians go to college or university (whether at home or abroad). In 2006 a new programme brought many secondary schools in line with international standards.

ANCIENT HISTORY

Archeological evidence suggests that human ancestors lived in the area that is now Mongolia 700,000 years ago. Experts believe that these ancient tribes began to migrate to different parts of the region around 20–30,000 years ago.

The first state, Hunnu, was officially established in 209 BC, and after this several other states existed for short periods of time. By 1206, Genghis Khan had united the clans and was recognised as the ruler of all the Mongols. At this time, the Mongol Empire included parts of China and Eurasia.

After Genghis Khan's death his successors continued the expansion of the empire. Genghis's grandson, Kublai Khan, established the Yuan Empire in 1260 and moved the capital to Dadu (now Beijing in China). The Yuan Empire was over-thrown by the Chinese Ming dynasty in 1368. After this, the last khan of the Yuan dynasty, Togoontumur, fled back to Mongolia.

In the fifteenth century, the Mongolian Empire began to disintegrate and its states became independent. The weakening of a once-powerful confederation provided an opportunity for other states to establish rule in the region. The Chinese Manchu Qin dynasty rose to prominence in the seventeenth century and over the following centuries – between 1691 and 1911 – brought Mongolia under its control.

RECENT HISTORY

Although Qin rule over Mongolia ended in 1911, the interests of neighbouring powers would not be served by allowing Mongolia to become a sovereign state. Despite this, in 1921, Mongolia proclaimed itself a republic under the control of the Soviets. In 1924 the Mongolian People's Republic was officially established, and China was forced to recognise Mongolia's *de facto* status.

The influence of the Soviets on Mongolia grew rapidly and the leaders of Mongolia became little more than puppets, forced to conform to Soviet policy. Steered by edicts from the Russian government, Mongolia set out on a path to socialist modernisation.

There were nationwide campaigns to make every individual literate and to educate young people in Marxist-Leninist (communist) doctrine. Programmes were also introduced to improve infrastructures such as healthcare and sanitation. Building programmes were launched and apartment blocks, schools, universities and factories were constructed. Increasing numbers of students attended universities and technical and vocational colleges. All citizens were guaranteed the right to employment. The Erdenet Mining Plant was opened, tapping one of the largest deposits of copper in the world. From this grew the third-largest city in the country.

In the wake of democratic reform, a monument of Soviet dictator Stalin is pulled down.

In 1920, around 20 per cent of the population lived in urban areas, while the rest continued the traditional nomadic lifestyle. The socialist era in Mongolia saw a dramatic rise in city-dwellers and today the balance has shifted so that only 15 to 20 per cent are herders.

In March 1990 the socialist government was overthrown and multi-party elections were held. By 1992 a new constitution had set Mongolia on the path to democracy.

CASE STUDY
DEMOCRATIC REVOLUTION

The winter of 1989 was characterised by rallies and demonstrations by the Mongolian people. Hundreds of thousands of people gathered to try and push through reform, and hunger strikes were held in an effort to topple the socialist government. In March the following year, the socialist Mongolian People's Revolutionary Party surrendered its monopoly.

With Mongolia's transition to democracy, foreign travel became possible for Mongolians and in turn many foreign countries established embassies there. International organisations also started to establish bases in Mongolia.

In July 1990 free elections were held for the first time, and young democratic political forces gained 40 per cent of the parliamentary seats. More importantly, presidential elections were held for the first time in Mongolia's history.

In 1992, Mongolia approved its new constitution, which renounced socialism. Four years later the MPRP – recorded in the *Guinness Book of Records* as the party in power for the longest period in history – took its seat as the opposition.

The mountain Tsambagarav is located in Hovd aimag.

Mongolia is located in the northern part of the continent of Asia. It has a total land area of 1,564,160 sq km, making it the nineteenth-largest country in the world. It is divided into areas of forest, mountains, steppe and desert.

THE GOBI DESERT

Approximately 20 per cent of Mongolia is covered by the Gobi Desert, in the southern part of the country. Five aimags lie in this region: Umnugobi (South Gobi), Dornogobi (East Gobi), Dundgobi (Central Gobi), Gobi Sumber and Gobi Altai.

Traces of dinosaur habitation in the desert millions of years ago are still being discovered, and the area is rich in rare and precious stones. Animals such as lizards, *mazalai* and *khavtgai* (a wild bactrian camel that is only found in Mongolia) also make their homes here. They have adapted to the Gobi's hot, dry climate and can go long periods without water.

Other regions of the Gobi have flat steppe as well as desert. Small wooded

The vast Gobi Desert covers one-fifth of the Mongolian landscape.

areas with water and prairie land form oases in the Gobi. In 1975 the Gobi region was declared a national park, which has offered greater protection for its rare flora and fauna. It is now the fourth-largest national park in the world.

STEPPE

Plains and steppe – semi-arid areas of grassy plains – cover the whole eastern part of Mongolia. The landscape here is more typical of the Asian continent than other parts of Mongolia. The steppe provides a habitat for many rare species, including marmots, wolves, gazelles and antelopes. (More than 70 per cent of the white-tailed gazelles in the country are found here.) There are also several unusual natural formations, including clusters of huge basalt columns found in the eastern and central parts of the country.

MOUNTAINS

Mountains, forests, rivers and creeks cover central, northern and western Mongolia. Compared to the Gobi region, these parts are much cooler. Almost all the northern aimags are included in this region. The mountains are divided into three main ranges: the Altai (both the longest and the highest), the Hangayn and the Hentiyn.

The region is rich with resources such as gold, lead, iron ore, precious stones and other raw materials. The mountains and rivers support fauna such as wild mountain sheep, ibex, boars, deer, brown antelopes, snow leopards, lynx, wolves, foxes, marmots and rabbits.

The northern Mongolian landscape is characterised by mountains and forests.

CASE STUDY
SAND STORMS

Mongolia suffers from severe sand storms (called *tuiren*) because of its vast desert area. These are most frequent in the spring months, and they can spread for hundreds of kilometres, causing widespread damage to property. They can also kill livestock, which can destroy the livelihoods of the nomadic peoples of the desert region. Some sand storms travel as far south as the northern provinces of China.

LAKE HUVSGUL

Lake Huvsgul is located in Huvsgul aimag between the two ports of Hatgal (in the north) and Khankh (in the south). It is the second-largest lake in Mongolia and the deepest freshwater lake not only in Mongolia but also in Central Asia. It contains 0.4 per cent of the world's freshwater. Lake Huvsgul is 136km long, 36km wide and 262m deep. It lies 1,645m above sea level. The lake is completely frozen between January until around April or the middle of May. Within the lake are several islands, including Dalain Khuis ('Oceanic Navel') and Khadan Khuis ('Rocky Navel'). Around the lake lie forests, but in recent years large parts of these have fallen victim to deforestation. Ninety-six rivers flow into the lake but only one – the River Eg – flows out of it. This joins with the River Selenge, which flows into Lake Baikal.

Lake Huvsgul is home to many varieties of fish, including white fish, lenok and sturgeon. In 1992 the lake became part of the Huvsgul Lake National Park. Five years later the area covering the Khoridol Saridag ridge was added to the national park, extending it by 838,000 hectares. The special protected area around Lake Huvsgul is the habitat of around 200 species of birds and animals such as wild mountain sheep, brown bears, moose and forest sable. Three ethnic groups – Buriats, Tsaatan (Reindeer People) and Darkhads – also live in this area.

Huvsgul is a vast freshwater reserve and the second-largest lake in Mongolia.

RIVERS

Mongolia has plenty of underground freshwater reserves – estimated at six billion cubic metres. These large freshwater reserves create great export potential for Mongolia, as amounts of freshwater are declining in many parts of the world.

Mongolian rivers flow into Arctic, Pacific and Central Asian river basins. There are more than 3,800 rivers in Mongolia, totalling 6,500km. The Orkhon is the longest river; other major rivers include the Selenge, Kerulen, Hovd and Dzavhan. The fast flow of these rivers means that there is potential for Mongolia to tap into the resource for hydroelectricity.

The River Chuluutiin, in Arkhangai aimag, has carved out beautiful natural formations in the area through which it flows.

CASE STUDY
WILDLIFE

The Mongolian *takhi* wild horse was discovered by the Russian scholar Przewalskii and is also known as Przewalskii's horse. In 1992 these animals were extinct in Mongolia but 16 of them were brought from Holland and reintroduced to their original habitat in Khustai Nuruu. The programme was successful and the population of *takhi* has now reached 200.

Snow leopards can be found throughout Central Asia, southern Siberia, the Mongol Altai Mountains, Khangai and Huvsgul. The *mazalai*, a species of bear unique to the Gobi, inhabits the small desert area to the south of the Mongol Altai. Although the *mazalai* looks similar to the brown bear, it can be identified by its longer limbs, and lighter, golden colouring. The *mazalai* is herbivorous and sleeps or hibernates in winter.

WEATHER

Mongolia has an extreme climate, with four distinct seasons. The sun shines for around 300 days of the year, although it is not always hot. Winter is long but dry, and temperatures range from -40°C in winter to 40°C in summer. Ulaanbaatar is the coldest capital city on Earth.

THE SEASONS

In Mongolia the cooler seasons last longer than the warmer ones. The cold weather usually begins in autumn and lasts until the end of spring. Summers are extremely hot and have become hotter over the past decade as the influence of of global warming is felt.

Spring begins in February and continues to around the middle of May. During this period, days become longer, nights grow shorter and average temperatures increase. Most animals wake up from their winter-long hibernation, and snow and frozen rivers melt. Spring in Mongolia is characterised by strong winds.

Throughout the summer months the herds gain strength and energy for the winter.

Summer lasts between 90 and 100 days from late May until September. It can rain heavily in the summer, but more often lack of rainfall causes droughts and poor harvests. Autumn begins in mid-September and lasts until early November. This is followed by a severe winter season.

Average low temperatures in Mongolia have been steadily increasing. Where once the winter average was -30⁰C, this was significantly higher by 2006.

Since ancient times, the Mongolians have divided the cold season into nine periods of nine days each, beginning on 22 December. This is known as the 'Coldness of Young Nine'. The middle three sets of nine days (27 days) are the coldest period. The end of this usually coincides with the New Year according to the lunar calendar.

TEMPERATURE

Temperatures in Mongolia drop to their lowest in January. In the Khangai region, temperatures can be as low as -35⁰C or -40⁰C. In June the temperature can rise to 35⁰C or 40⁰C in some places. In 1966 Mongolia suffered an extremely severe winter – the coldest in recorded history – with temperatures as low as -60⁰C.

In general the river-basin regions are the coldest places in winter (in the Lake Uvs area in the west, the temperature can drop to -58⁰C). The hottest region is Khanbogd *soum* (district), in Umnugobi aimag in southern Mongolia. Here, temperatures can reach 50⁰C. In the Gobi Desert temperatures of 40⁰C are common in summer. The weather in Ulaanbaatar is extremely hot, especially during the national festival held there in July.

Over the last 64 years, annual average temperatures in Mongolia have increased: average temperatures in spring and autumn by 1.3⁰C to 1.8⁰C; in summer by 0.5⁰C; and in winter by 3.6⁰C.

WIND

Mongolia's unique geographical location means that its weather can be harsh and unpredictable. Strong winds can stir up severe dust and sand storms, and although winds are strongest in spring they occur throughout the year, blowing mainly from the west and north. Although wind speeds are rarely more than one metre per second in the lowland regions, they can reach speeds of two to five metres per second in the more open steppe regions. Very high winds – with speeds of up to 15 metres per second – have been known. Blizzards are a characteristic of the winter months and last for between one and six hours. The windiest area is Mandalgobi, in Dundgobi aimag. Here, wind speeds have reached 40 metres per second.

Many Mongolians live in temporary shelters called *ghers,* which can be very cold. Wood is thus an important fuel in winter.

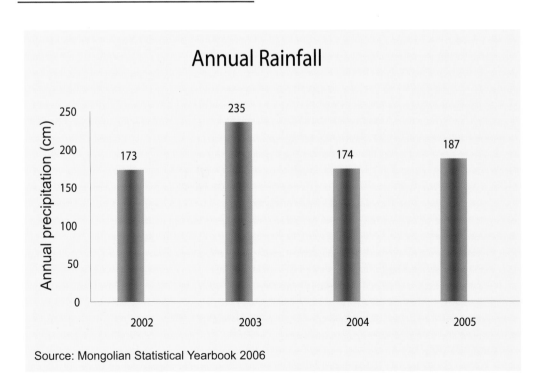

Source: Mongolian Statistical Yearbook 2006

Mongolia has a young population – more than a quarter are children under 15.

At the beginning of the twentieth century, the population of Mongolia was estimated to be between 500,000 and 700,000. By 2007, however, the population had reached over 2.6 million. The people are divided by cultural traditions into different groups, the largest of which is the Khalkha.

THE PEOPLE OF MONGOLIA

Small groups of people have inhabited this vast region since ancient times, but its population has always been low in relation to its size. At the turn of the twentieth century, there were still fewer than one million people living in Mongolia. The twentieth century saw a rapid population growth, however, as the country gained independence and started its programme of modernisation. In middle of the century, the government began to encourage nomadic groups to settle in the cities, and the country is now much more urbanised than ever before.

The campaign for cultural improvement implemented by the government also had a significant impact on population growth. By the 1980s, the population had reached 1.7 million. The economic reforms of the early 1990s resulted in a brief population decline (although by then it had reached 2.1 million). It began to increase again as the 1990s progressed. By the end of the century the population was 2.4 million and by 2005, 2.5 million. This increase looks set to continue well into the twenty-first century – estimates suggest that it will increase by 1.46 per cent each year.

POPULATION STRUCTURE
The ratio of men and women in Mongolia is almost equal – women make up 49.9 per cent and men account for 50.1 per cent of the population. Divided into age categories, 27.9 per cent of the population is between 0 and 14 years old; people between 15 and 64 make up 68.4 per cent; and those over 65, 3.7 per cent. Average life expectancy for women is 67.8 and 61.6 for men. The birth rate is 18.3 per 1,000 of the population – below the world average of 20.3.

DENSITY AND DISTRIBUTION
The traditional Mongolian way of life was nomadic: widely dispersed tribes travelled across the country making their living from livestock herding. There was little focus in large settlemements. As Mongolia modernised in the twentieth century, cities expanded as increasing numbers were attracted to urban areas. Today, almost half the population lives in just one city – Ulaanbaatar. This trend is likely to continue because most universities, colleges, factories and job opportunities are focused in the capital.

While Ulaanbaatar still attracts the most people, other cities are also growing rapidly – places like Darkhan and Erdenet are now major urban areas with high population densities. Erdenet in particular began increasing in popularity in the 1970s, when the mining plant was established. Large numbers of people are attracted to the cities by the prospect of earning a better living than they can in rural areas.

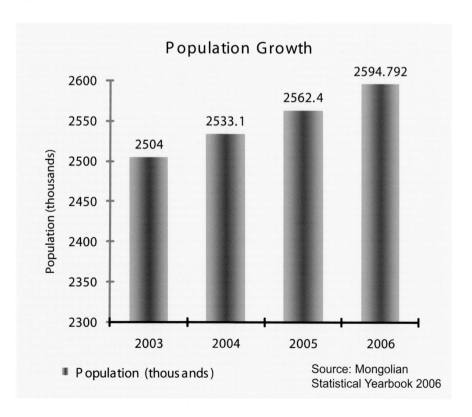

Source: Mongolian Statistical Yearbook 2006

As increasing numbers of people move to the cities, the traditional nomadic way of life, herding stock animals, is suffering. This rapid concentration in urban centres and the decline in countryside populations has raised concerns among some groups, who fear that ancient traditions may be lost forever.

ETHNIC GROUPS

A number of different ethnic groups are spread out across Mongolia. Among these are the Khalkha Mongols (94.9 per cent of the population) and Kazakhs (5 per cent). Other ethnic groups account for 0.1 per cent of the population, and include the Durvod, Zakhchin, Urianhay, Oold, Tsaatan, Bayad, Tsakhar, Myangad, Monchoor, Khoton, Buriat, Torguud, Darkhad and Oirad.

Each of these groups has its own distinct costumes, traditions, culture, religious beliefs and language or dialects. For example, the Oolds, who live in Khovd aimag, have different names for certain items, which makes it difficult for people from other groups to understand their conversation. The Buryats can be found in both Russia and Mongolia. Russian Buryats have their own republics, while

Kazakh men hunting with their eagles.

in Mongolia they are focused in small settlements in particular areas. After the Russian Revolution in 1917, many Buryats there moved into and settled in Mongolia. Buryats now reside in Khentii, Dornod and Bulgan aimags.

The Kazakhs live in the northwestern aimag of Bayan-Ulgii and speak a distinct Kazakh language. Unlike other ethnic groups in Mongolia, they do not observe the Tsagaan sar festival (see page 28), but they celebrate the New Year holiday.

The Tsaatans – Reindeer People – live in the taiga and forest regions of Huvsgul aimag. They are among the few groups who have not migrated to the cities. Instead they still live in huts, as they have done for centuries.

FOREIGN SETTLERS

Many foreigners have now obtained Mongolian citizenship – mostly by marrying Mongolian subjects. Currently, there are significant numbers of Russian and Chinese settlers in Mongolia.

During the socialist period in the early twentieth century, many young people went to study in Russia. They often married Russians before moving with their families back to Mongolia. Many of

Since ancient times, a variety of ethnic groups have lived in the western aimags.

The main transport of the Tsaatan is reindeer, but in recent years the number of reindeer in the country has significantly decreased.

these people and their descendants still live there. At the same time, many Russians were invited to work in Mongolia, and they also married Mongolian citizens and made the country their home.

During the centuries of Chinese rule over Mongolia, thousands of Chinese settled in Mongolia. Although many later returned to China, others stayed and made Mongolia their permanent home.

MIGRATION

Internal migration intensified throughout the 1990s. With the introduction of the market reform, many state-owned factories closed and thousands of people found themselves unemployed. They began their own businesses in an effort to improve their quality of life. This situation greatly contributed to migration.

While rural residents are now moving to the cities, many urban dwellers also aspire to move abroad either to work or study. Since 2000, large numbers of Mongolians have been living abroad. An unofficial estimate suggests that there are around 200,000 Mongolians now living in other countries. A significant portion of these have settled in South Korea, which offers higher incomes.

Mongolians have also migrated to the United States, where they concentrate in major cities such as San Francisco, Chicago, Denver and Los Angeles. Other countries to which Mongolians have moved include Great Britain, Japan, China, Russia, the Czech Republic, Hungary, Ireland and Germany. They have been driven there by unemployment and low salaries in their own country.

Tibetan Buddhism was adopted in Mongolia 400 years ago.

RELIGION

Historically, Mongolians were followers of Shamanism. Even in the days of the Empire, when they came into contact with and conquered other cultures, they maintained their Shamanist beliefs. In the ninth century Buddhism began to infiltrate Mongolia from the region that is now Afghanistan. In the fifteenth to sixteenth centuries, the Mongolian Empire dissolved and many members of the ruling class began to search for a philosophy that might help reunite the country. Buddhist teachings met their requirements and from this time Tibetan Buddhism began to spread more rapidly and became the dominant religion. Within a few years, other religions gained a following in Mongolia, including Christianity and Islam. The decline of Shamanism was largely encouraged by the Chinese Manchu rulers.

RELIGION TODAY

Today, around 50 per cent of Mongolians are Buddhists or follow Shamanism. Christians and Muslims make up around six per cent. Although Buddhism spread hundreds of years ago, the socialist regime purged such beliefs and embraced an atheist doctrine, resulting in the large numbers that today still profess no religious affiliation (around 40 per cent).

Other than these major religions, however, there are numerous religious sects and denominations finding their way into Mongolia. For example, Christian denominations such as Mormons are spreading their beliefs through the establishment of missionaries in the country. Despite this, Buddhism still dominates. The Tibetan Dalai Lama has visited Mongolia four times since 1978 and each visit has increased pressures from China, which now rules Tibet.

Mongolians have always followed a policy of religious tolerance, proving to the world that it is possible for different religions to peacefully coexist. The earliest travellers to the Mongolian Empire – including Marco Polo – witnessed this, and it is still evident today. Monks, missionaries and mullahs could recite their teachings and prayers, and worship in their own way, without fear of reprisal. The Mongolian rulers proclaimed that all religions were equal and strictly enforced this rule.

EDUCATION

In Mongolia, children go to kindergarden at the age of three, and school at the age of six. Education is compulsory for 10 years. Students can choose to go to university or college at the age of 18.

Mongolia is slowly transforming its education system to meet world standards.

CASE STUDY
NATIONAL UNIVERSITY OF MONGOLIA

The National University of Mongolia is the oldest in the country. It was established in 1942 and in 1946 the first 35 students graduated from NUM. Today it has 12 colleges and trains more than 10,000 students in fields such as languages, literature, science, journalim, geography, fine art, and history. They are taught by some of Mongolia's most renowned scholars and teachers.

Publicly run secondary schools were established in Mongolia in 1940 and the number of them rapidly increased. Now there are more than 100, as well as an increasing number of private secondary schools. Public schools are run according to a curriculum established by the Ministry of Education and do not charge any tuition fees. Parents have to pay for their children to attend private schools, however. Private schools are not subject to government authority.

There are also state-owned and private colleges and universities. State-owned universities outnumber the private ones. During the socialist era, students could study at universities free of charge or were given grants. After the fall of socialism and the rise of democracy, however, a system was introduced by which people had to pay tuition fees for a place at university, and this system is still in place.

Although the existing universities – including the National University of Mongolia – offer courses in many different professional fields, there is still a lack of training available in some specialist areas. As a result, many young people still choose to study abroad, and in particular receive their postgraduate degrees overseas. There are many opportunities for Mongolians to study at universities in Japan, China, Russia, the United States, the United Kingdom, Turkey, Vietnam and South Korea.

HEALTHCARE

After the democratic and market reform in the late twentieth century, the healthcare system in Mongolia experienced both successes and failures. One of the greatest achievements after the fall of Communism was the establishment of many private clinics and hospitals, offering higher standards of healthcare than had previously been available. However, training for doctors in Mongolia is not widely available and

The Mongolian constitution stipulates that citizens have the right to live freely wherever they choose. Under the socialist regime, people who lived in the countryside were not permitted to move to the cities. However, after its collapse, all citizens were allowed to move around and settle in cities, on payment of a small fee. This decision was repealed in 2005 and rural citizens can now settle in cities without having to pay. Since this repeal, there has been a sharp increase in migration to urban areas. In the last two decades especially, living conditions in rural areas have declined as the lack of employment opportunities in the countryside has driven rural residents to the cities to earn a better living.

In most cases, new immigrants to the city live in *gher* districts.

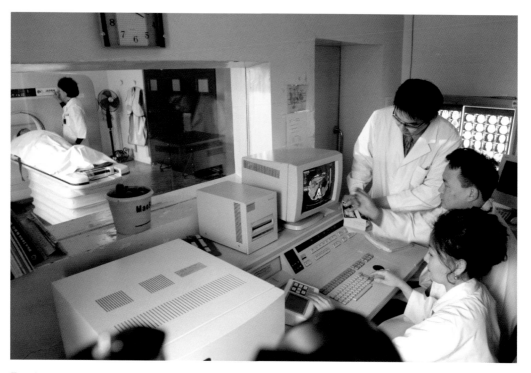

Rapid developments in technology and equipment in the Mongolian health sector have taken place in recent years.

there is a lack of qualified practitioners and readily available medicines.

The government pays for healthcare for children up to the age of 16. After this, individuals are responsible for having health insurance to cover any healthcare costs. Employers sometimes offer this is as part of an employment package. However, there are thousands of people who cannot afford health insurance and who suffer as a result of the lack of a public health scheme.

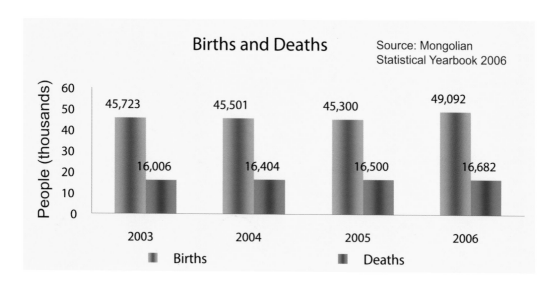

Births and Deaths   Source: Mongolian Statistical Yearbook 2006

NATIONAL HOLIDAYS

NAADAM

One of the best-known festivals in Mongolia is Naadam, also known as 'The Three Manly Games', and it has been celebrated for centuries. It begins on 11 July and although the largest celebration takes place in Ulaanbaatar, smaller Naadam festivals are held throughout the country. The 'Three Manly Games' of its name are horse-racing, archery and wrestling, and the festival consists of competitions in these three events. In the past the games served as a form of military training for young men, as well as an opportunity for the widely dispersed people of Mongolia to gather together. By the mid-seventeenth century Naadam was being held every three years, but in 1772 it became an annual event. The significance attached to the festival has varied over the centuries, although it has retained its basic format, but it is now an official state holiday celebrating Mongolian independence. Today, the sporting standards in each event are of a highly professional level.

In the past, to train for the horse-racing, herders would prepare their horses for up to a month before Naadam, only allowing children to ride them. Soon a group of people developed who were specialists in this kind of training, and they developed different breeds of racehorses ideally suited to the conditions demanded by the festival. Because horses had long been the closest companions of the nomadic Mongols, they were regarded with great respect. Those that won the

Over the course of the two days of the Naadam festival, either 512 or 1,024 wrestlers compete and a champion is determined.

The horse-racing events take place on a long course with many curves, so spectators can only watch from the finish line.

race were highly prized and awarded medals. Those that won on more than one occasion were given special additional names (often relating to their unique characteristics such as colouring). Monuments were even dedicated to these distinguished horses.

Today, the horse-races are divided into six classes, organised by age. One of the most popular races of the festival is that of the four-year-olds. It is traditionally believed that the dust kicked up by the galloping of horses of this age brings luck and happiness.

The horse that finishes last in the two-year-old class (the *daaga* class) is given the title *Bayan Khodood* ('Rich Stomach') and a special award, in the belief that that horse will do better in the next race.

The horse-racing events are unusual in that all the jockeys are children – usually aged between seven and 12.

Wrestling is a popular national sport in Mongolia, and this is one of the three main games during Naadam. Usually 512 wrestlers compete over the course of the festival, but on special anniversaries of the celebration this number is doubled.

There are no age and weight categories in national wrestling. The various titles are awarded on the basis of the wrestler's success in the annual Naadam contest. Titles of wrestlers are usually the names of birds or animals, symbolising their strength and shrewdness. The highest title is Champion and the lowest title is the Hawk. The wrestlers meet in a single elimination tournament that lasts nine or ten rounds. It is unique to Mongolian wrestling that those participants with higher titles get to choose their opponents.

Archery is the third event in the Naadam festival, and the only one in

In contrast with the other two games, archery is the only discipline that welcomes competitors of any age and sex.

which women are allowed to compete. It is thought that in the earliest days of the festival, competitors would shoot at a hanging target while riding on horseback. Later, under the Chinese Manchu rulers, the target was changed into a *Khasaa* – a small ball-shaped item knitted with hide straps. As Naadam developed, bows and arrows turned from weapons into sports equipment, fashioned out of birch or bamboo, ibex or deer horns and animal tendons, bound together with a glue made from animal hide and fish bladders.

The bows used in Naadam are much smaller than the bows once used by Mongolians in warfare. The arrows have feathers at the end and the arrowheads are made of bone rather than metal.

In the course of the archery competition, men must fire 40 arrows from 75 metres away from the target, while women fire 20 arrows from 60 metres away. The person with the most target hits wins the tournament. There are no age restrictions in the archery contest – children are allowed to participate – and there are both individual and group contents. The winners are granted the titles of 'National Marksman' and 'National Markswoman'.

All the participants in the games – archers, horse-trainers and wrestlers – are officially granted a title by the government of Mongolia and they each have their own special hats decorated with different signs and emblems.

TSAGAAN SAR

Like other Asian nations, Mongolia follows the lunar calendar (rather than the solar calendar commonly used in the West). The lunar New Year, known as Tsagaan sar ('White Moon') in Mongolia, is usually celebrated in February. Since the spread of Tibetan Buddhism into Mongolia, and the country's adoption of the Tibetan calendar methodology, the exact dates of the New Year do not always correspond with those of China, Japan and other Asian nations.

Just as it in in the Western calendar, New Year's Eve is important and is widely celebrated. The moon cannot be seen on New Year's Eve, so the day is referred to as *Bituun*, which means 'to close down'. According to Tibetan Buddhist mythology, on the eve of the New Year, the god Baldanlham visits every family. People leave pieces of ice on top of their *ghers* for his thirsty horse to drink. On *Bituun*, families prepare a great feast. Foods such as lamb and beef are eaten as part of this feast. Layers of biscuits cooked in special shapes are made into a 'cake' with an odd number of tiers. People also often make and freeze large amounts of other traditional dishes such as *buuz* (a type of steamed dumpling filled with mutton or beef), so that they can be brought out and shared whenever guests visit during this time of celebration.

The New Year begins with the sunrise after New Year's Eve. According to Buddhist thought, the first day indicates how the whole year will be. Therefore, people often get up before sunrise – as prescribed by the Buddhist horoscope – and they pray and carry out other customs. It is considered important to start this day in the right way to ensure good luck for the whole year.

As the sun rises, the greeting ceremony starts within the immediate family. Younger family members greet older ones by extending their arms to support their elders beneath the elbows. They exchange words of greeting and good wishes. Usually young people give *khadag* – a blue or white strip of finely woven silk – or sometimes banknotes. The older family members offer gifts in exchange.

The greeting ceremony is later shared with extended family. Husbands and wives and pregnant women do not greet one another. It is said that if pregnant women participate in the greeting ceremony, then the gender of the child may change.

Many of the old traditions of Tsagaan sar have been preserved, particularly in rural households. However, as more and more Mongolians move to the towns and cities, the customs of the New Year festival are changing. For example, in urban areas, the festival ends after five days (elsewhere it may last for up to seven days). However, during this time, people still dress up in the national costume both in the countryside and cities.

During Tsagaan sar, Mongolians are forbidden to argue with one another. Any old disputes must be forgiven and forgotten during this period, and all debts must be repaid by the time the festival is celebrated.

A table set for Tsagaan sar, with layers of traditional biscuits.

AGRICULTURE, TRADE AND INDUSTRY

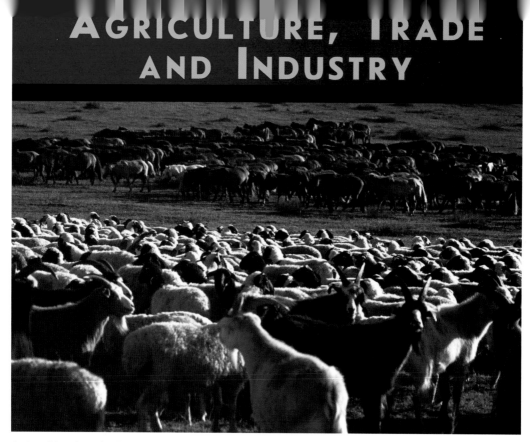

Animal husbandry has been the traditional form of farming for centuries.

Raising livestock has long been Mongolia's key industry, and large areas of the country are given over to animal husbandry. There are around 30 million animals, although this varies in times of drought or during particularly harsh winters. Recently, intensive livestock farming has been introduced in some areas.

LIVESTOCK FARMING

Herders are people who make their livings by raising and herding animals. As recently as 100 years ago almost all Mongolians were herders, but this changed during the twentieth century. The nature of the land meant that most Mongolians led a nomadic lifestyle – moving from place to place to find the best pastures for feeding and breeding their livestock.

As the numbers of people working in animal husbandry decreased, it was suggested that more intensive livestock farming should be introduced. If farmers only have small herds, they are at risk of losing everything in a severe winter or a long, drought-ridden summer. This is their only livelihood – they sell the animal's meat, milk, hide and wool.

CASHMERE

Goats play an important part in Mongolian animal husbandry, and more than 30 per cent of the total livestock in the country is goats. Bayankhongor aimag has more goat herds than anywhere else. Their significance lies with the production of cashmere, which is made from goats' wool. This is softer than the wool of other animals and has very thin fibres, which can be made into high-quality cashmere.

Cashmere is harvested by combing goats once a year in spring. It is estimated that 300g to 500g of cashmere can be collected from a cashmere goat and 150g to 300g from an ordinary goat. Cashmere jumpers, scarves, hats, gloves, T-shirts and socks are all made in Mongolia and exported to other countries. Raw cashmere wool or wool that has already been processed into cashmere is also exported.

Wool and cashmere products make up a significant amount of Mongolia's export goods, which is why there are thousands more head of goats and sheep than there are of other animals. Mongolia is second only to China in its cashmere exports. Every year approximately 3,000 tonnes of cashmere is harvested and around 70 per cent of it is processed domestically. Cashmere production accounts for 7.5 per cent of gross domestic product (GDP) and there are around 80 domestic and foreign-invested companies that process the wool.

CONSUMER PRODUCTS

Mongolians produce many consumer products made from the milk, meat, hide and wool of their livestock, which includes sheep, cows, camels and horses as well as goats.

Yoghurt, cream, dried curds and butter are all made from cow's milk.

Cashmere is one of Mongolia's main export goods.

These dairy products are either prepared by the livestock farmers or in factories. A traditional drink, *airag*, is made from fermented horse's milk. The fresh milk is poured into a special skin bag, where it is kept and repeatedly stirred. Bulgan aimag is particularly well-known for its *airag*.

Mongolians mostly eat mutton (meat from adult sheep), especially during the Tsagaan sar festival. Other meats, such as goat, beef, camel and horse, are also widely consumed and their hides and wool are processed. The wool and cashmere-processing industries have developed rapidly in recent years as demand for these products increases in other countries.

THE SPREAD OF AGRICULTURE

Agriculture has not spread widely in Mongolia, largely because of the climate, which does not support crop farming in many areas. Nevertheless, during the socialist era, with the assistance of the Soviet Union, the agriculture industry and crop farming were intensively developed as part of the state's policies. Many collective farms (those owned by the state) were established. The success of this programme was proven by the fact that Mongolia produced enough of some agricultural goods to export to the Soviet Union.

Today, however, Mongolia's agriculture industry is unable to support its domestic demand, and the country imports many of its agricultural goods – including flour, vegetables, fruit and grain – from China. Despite this, there are several farms in operation, most notably in Selenge, Tuv and Orkhon aimags. The industry is gradually recovering, however. In 2005, for example, Mongolia harvested 64,200 tonnes of vegetables – a significant increase from previous years.

Agriculture was intensively developed in Mongolia in the 1960s under the influence of the Soviet regime.

The city of Erdenet grew up around the mining plant established there in 1978.

IMPORT AND EXPORT

Mongolia imports most of its consumer goods. Vegetables, clothing and electronic products are imported from China and the countries of Southeast Asia. This huge volume of imports from its southern neighbours is linked to the decline of small and medium-sized enterprises in Mongolia. China and other countries are able to produce many goods at a much lower cost than Mongolia.

Apart from cashmere and wool, Mongolia's main export is metal, particularly copper. The country has one of the largest reserves of copper in the world. In 2005 it exported 587,100 tonnes of copper concentrate to the world markets.

The textile industry is also on the rise, and in the late 1990s a number of foreign textile companies joined with those in Mongolia to establish large textile factories, which now supply clothes to countries such as the United States.

In recent times, commercial banks have started offering low interest-rate loans to promote small and medium-sized businesses, which will help develop Mongolia's export industry further.

INDUSTRY

With the collapse of the socialist regime the Mongolian industry sector seemed doomed to failure. However, as political and economic stability returned to the country, an industrial sector based on mineral resources began to develop.

COAL

Coal that can be made into coke accounts for 20 per cent of an estimated total of 150 billion tonnes of coal reserves in Mongolia, although coking coal is rarely

Tavan Tolgoi – one of the richest coal deposits in the world – is located in Umnugobi aimag.

Over the last few years, the number of gold mines in Mongolia has increased and gold accounts for significant portion of mining products.

used in Mongolian industry. Mongolian power plants burn bitumous rather than coking coal to generate electricity, so the demand for this resource is not high in the country itself. Instead, most of the coking coal mined here is exported to China. This type of coal burns with a very high temperature, so it is widely used in China's processing plants. The Tavan Tolgoi coal mine in Umnugobi aimag is one of the richest in the world.

Coal production is increasing every year, as there is increasing demand for the resource to burn in power plants, and the many people who live in the *gher* settlements rely on coal for heating in the cold winters. In 2003, 5,666,100 tonnes of coal were extracted; in 2005, this figure increased to 7,517,100 tonnes. Although coking coal is largely exported, other types are used domestically in high volumes.

The major coal deposits are found at Nalaikh and Baganuur (both close to Ulaanbaatar) and Shariin Gol. The Nalaikh deposit was discovered by accident when a child found what he thought was a black stone while out playing. The Chinese in the region established the first coal mine. Almost all aimags have their own coal mines, but coal is also shipped to other areas.

COPPER

In the late 1960s, Czech geologists working in Mongolia discovered a large copper deposit in Bulgan aimag. Copper reserves are now estimated at 1.3 billion tonnes. The copper and molybdenum concentrates that are used for export are only extracted from the Erdenet Mining Plant, and Mongolia exports approximately 580,000 tonnes of copper concentrate every year.

A further gold and copper deposit was later discovered in the Khanbogd district of Umnugobi aimag. The Oyu Tolgoi reserve has three times the amount of copper found at Erdenet, and there are discussions underway about how best to utilise and manage this valuable resource for the country's benefit.

The Erdenet Mining Plant was established in 1978 as a joint Mongolian-Russian venture. It alone constitutes half of foreign trade and 25 per cent of domestic income from these resources. This plant extracts its ore through placer mining (a form of surface or open-cast mining). It has very high running and production costs, and suffers from a lack of competitive advantage and outdated equipment. Production efficiency, technology and output need to be increased and improved in order to benefit the economy further.

GOLD

Mongolia is rich with gold deposits. These can be found in Bayankhongor aimag, Selenge aimag and the Zaamar district of Tuv aimag. At the beginning of the twentieth century there were several gold-extraction companies in the Bayankhongor and Yeroo river basins as well as in the Khangai, Khentii and Baidrag areas. Today, gold is mined in Baidrag, Bugant, Ikh Altat, Sharyn Gol, Zaamar, Boroo and Narantolgoi.

More than half of Mongolia's gold is produced by seven key mines. The other half is extracted by a collection of smaller mines in the various regions. There are around 150 mines in all. Some of these are domestic, others function through foreign investment, and some are joint ventures. In territorial terms, around 40 per cent of the total amount of gold is extracted in Tuv, and 35 per cent from Selenge, Darkhan-Uul and Arkhangai aimags.

CASE STUDY
GOLD MINING

Mining gold manually (by hand), is not a traditional Mongolian method. It can be risky to conduct such mining without any scientific research or proper authorisation. However, manual gold mining is still practised in the gold regions.

Individuals will go to areas where gold deposits are known and search the soil that has been dug up. They use mercury to separate the gold from the soil and water. Direct contact with mercury can be dangerous and causes health problems. The number of hand-miners was estimated to be more than 50,000 in 2003.

The foundations of light industry were laid during the socialist era.

CRUDE OIL

Oil prospecting began in Mongolia in the 1940s. Up until this time the country had imported its oil and petroleum, but in the mid-1950s oil was discovered in Zuunbayan, in Dornogobi aimag, and extraction of this precious resource began. By 1969, however, the reserves of oil here had been severely depleted and the government ordered the closure of the wells. Once again, Mongolia had to import its oil.

In 1997, a major oil deposit was discovered in the Tamsag basin in the east of the country. Nowadays, crude oil is mined both here and in Zuunbayan, and exported in its crude form. This crude oil is extracted and directly exported to China. In 1999, 71,600 barrels of oil were exported. By 2005 this number had increased to 188,100.

ZINC

There is a zinc mine located in Tumurtei, in Sukhbaatar aimag. This mine was established in 2005 and is jointly operated by China and Mongolia.

FLUORITE

Fluorite is used in the manufacture of metals and glass. Fluorite deposits are found in three main areas in Mongolia, located in the north and south of the country, as well as a seam that crosses east to west. Among these, the horizontal zone has the largest reserves. The biggest fluorite mine is located at Bor-Undur, in Khentii aimag. This mine is estimated to contain six million tonnes of fluorite ore. There are six fluorite mines in all, and the Russian-Mongolian joint venture Monrostsvet Corporation owns four of these. Mongolia is the fourth-largest

As mining productivity increases in Mongolia, so too do environmental concerns.

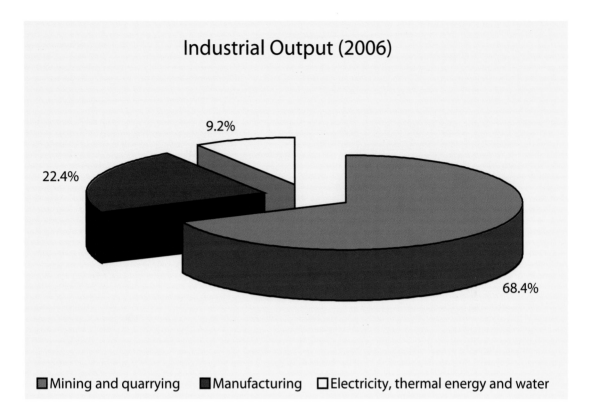

Industrial Output (2006)

9.2%

22.4%

68.4%

- ■ Mining and quarrying
- ■ Manufacturing
- □ Electricity, thermal energy and water

producer of fluorite concentrate in the world, exporting mainly to countries such as Russia, Moldavia, Japan and the countries of the European Union.

FOOD INDUSTRY

Mongolia produces meat, milk, flour, fruit and vegetables. Many of these are produced to satisfy domestic demand, but they still have to compete with imports.

The most developed food industries in Mongolia are those that produce alcoholic drinks, flour and meat products. Only the drinks industry provides a significant percentage of GDP every year. The government receives several billion tugriks in tax returns from this industry.

As state-owned enterprises were privatised after the fall of the Soviet regime, more factories were built around the food industry. Despite the success of privatisation, many food products must still be imported to meet demand.

SERVICE INDUSTRY

With all the changes taking place in Mongolia in the mid-1990s, the country realised the importance of improving its service industry in order to enhance the economy. In recent years the service industry has improved dramatically, opening up more job opportunities and also helping the country manage areas such as tourism more efficiently.

INFORMATION TECHNOLOGY

Information technology is the fastest-growing sector in Mongolia. In 2006, the government launched a programme intended to provide a computer for every household in the country. Part of this programme involved eliminating the import tax on computers so that families could afford to buy high-quality hardware at a reasonable price.

Internet use has also increased. There are around 10 Internet service providers,

Internet access is now available to many Mongolians.

supplying both wired and wireless Internet access. From the mid-1990s Internet cafes have been springing up and hundreds of them now provide Internet and email facilities for those who do not yet have home computers.

TELECOMMUNICATIONS

Mongolian Telecommunication LLC was the first Mongolian telephone company and it still monopolises the market. The company operates around 160,000 phones.Communication has improved over the past decade, even in some of the more remote parts of the country.

Currently, three mobile-phone companies operate in Mongolia: MobiCom, SkyTel and UniTel. The first of these was MobiCom and it is now the largest of the three, with around 550,000 subscribers. The companies use two different systems, GSM and CDMA. One in three people in Mongolia owns a mobile phone.

TOURISM INDUSTRY

Mongolia's history as a region of people who relied on livestock and nomadic farming ensured that for centuries its wild

beauty remained unspoilt. Even with the spread of urban areas, there are still vast swathes of land in Mongolia that are untouched by human activity.

Every year, increasing numbers of tourists visit to admire the scenery of the sand dunes in the Gobi Desert, Lake Huvsgul, the Altai Mountain range and the Altan Ovoo and Terelj national parks. The Tsenher hot spring – with temperatures of around 86^0C – in Arkhangai aimag also attracts tourists from within Mongolia and abroad. Gorhi-Terelj national park is located 50km from Ulaanbaatar and is famous for its unique rock formations and rare plants.

The tourism industry has developed intensively since the mid-1990s. As relationships improve with other countries, more and more people are considering Mongolia as a holiday destination. In 2003 the government announced the Year of Visiting Mongolia and 2006 was the 800th Anniversary of the Great Mongolian State.

CULTURE AND HISTORICAL TOURISM

As Buddhism spread throughout Mongolia, numerous temples and monasteries were built. Many of these were destroyed during the purges of 1937. One of the few remaining is Amarbayasgalant monastery located in Baruun buren *soum*, in Selenge aimag. The monastery was founded in 1727 by the Manchu emperor and comprises 40 temples. These include those of Ayush, Mahagala, Maitriya, Narkhajid, Bogd Jivzundamba, Zanabazar.

In 2006, the Mongolia Project was begun in Tsonjin Boldog to build a monument to Genghis Khan, surrounded by the *ghers* of Mongolian clans. This was intended to show how Mongolians lived in the thirteenth century. Both the monastery and the Mongolia Project have become popular tourist attractions.

ADVENTURE TOURISM

Adventure tourism is also popular among visitors to Mongolia. In particular, horse-riding holidays are arranged, which allow tourists to enjoy the landscape on horse-back. This offers a good opportunity to learn more about the country and the historical nomadic lifestyle, as well as take in the breathtaking scenery.

CASE STUDY
KHARAKORUM

The ruins of Kharakorum, the capital city of the old Mongolian Empire, are located in Uvurkhangai aimag. As well as being the capital city, this was also a place where both foreign and domestic travellers, envoys and merchants stopped on their journeys.

According to historical records there was a fountain here, with four heads each facing a different direction. This fountain was created by a French sculptor. Legend has it that each head would pour a different liquid: vodka, *airag*, milk and honey.

The ruins of Kharakorum city are not extensive, but items from the area have been uncovered by an international team of archeologists. The Erdenezuu monastery was built over the ruins, and can still be seen.

The number of tourists visiting Mongolia is increasing every year, bringing a valuable source of revenue to the country.

TRANSPORT, ENERGY AND THE ENVIRONMENT

Mongolians once travelled by horse. Now railways allow easy cross-country travel.

The Mongolian government has taken environmental concerns seriously, and it is attempting to develop the country's infrastructure in a way that addresses environmental issues. Despite this, pollution remains a problem, particularly in Ulaanbaatar.

TRANSPORT

AIR TRANSPORT

International flights out of Mongolia are run by the state-owned MIAT company. It runs regular flights to Germany, Russia, South Korea, China and Japan. The Genghis Khan International Airport (previously known as Buyant Ukhaa) is located in Ulaanbaatar. There are 44 airports in total across Mongolia.

Numbers of travellers using air transport have increased in recent years. In 2005 around 300,000 domestic and international passengers were served by the national carrier. The majority of these passengers are foreign tourists; the rest are Mongolians travelling within the country.

Although MIAT once controlled domestic flights, these were privatised in early 2000 and the company Aero Mongolia took over. In 2006 another private company, EZNIS Airways, began running a domestic flight service.

RAIL TRANSPORT

There are 1,810km of railways in Mongolia. These connect the north and south of the country, running through the capital Ulaanbaatar. The railroads are owned and run by a joint Mongolian-Russian venture.

Rail travel is one of the most popular forms of transport in Mongolia, and people use the trains to travel between local destinations. The number of train passengers reached 4.2 million in 2005 – a sharp increase from previous years.

The railroads also transport around 90 per cent of Mongolia's total export and import goods out of and into the country.

Half the air transport in Mongolia is owned and run by private companies.

ROAD TRANSPORT

Mongolian roads run to a total length of 49,250km. Around 1,724km of this is paved but the rest is unpaved.

In 2000 a project called Millennium Road was launched. This is a plan to build a road connecting the west and the east of the country, and the north to the south. The project is being funded by both domestic and international contributions. Although this is a vast undertaking, it has been criticised because it still does not connect all the aimags.

The amount of road traffic has increased in the twenty-first century, as more and more Mongolians own their own cars. In 2005, there were more than 131,000 cars in the country. This has contributed to the rise in pollution levels.

Although private car use is on the increase, taxis still operate in urban areas.

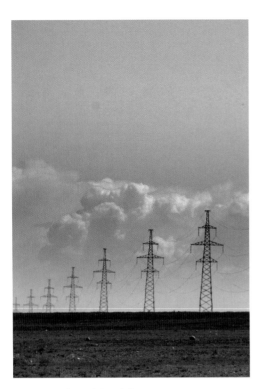

Most rural residential areas are connected to the central electricity grid.

ENERGY

During the socialist era, Mongolia bought some of its electricity from the Soviet Union. Today, the country is attempting to supply its own domestic needs, and the energy industry aims to supply affordable and consistent electricity to the majority of Mongolians. Despite this, many areas – particularly the *gher* districts – are often cut off from a power supply. The energy sector has been operating on a deficit for many years. One solution to this problem is to privatise the industry, but even so, many issues will still need to be addressed.

POWER SUPPLY

The electricity network is focused in Ulaanbaatar, Darkhan, Erdenet and Choibalsan. This delivers electricity to 18 aimags, and approximately 170 *soum* districts. Three aimags and 150 *soums* are not connected to the central electricity grid.

THERMAL POWER

Thermal power stations play a crucial role in Mongolian energy supply, generating both electricity and heat. Smaller thermal power plants have been used to provide energy in some areas for a number of years, and their use is increasing.

FUEL

All Mongolia's power plants are fuelled by bituminous coal. Although the country has large reserves of coal, it is still an expensive form of fuel, increasing the cost of private and commercial energy, and causing environmental damage.

Coal for the power plants is transported from the Nalaikh, Baganuur and Sharyn Gol mines. Around 7,000,000 tonnes of coal are burned by the plants every year and this rate of consumption is increasing.

Coal is also used as a fuel in private households. Thousands of families, particularly those living in *ghers*, have to burn coal to heat their homes as they have no heating systems.

HYDROELECTRIC POWER

The first hydroelectric power plant in Mongolia was built by the Chinese in

Hydroelectric power is becoming increasingly popular in Mongolia, harnessing a renewable resource.

Erecting a small hydroelectric station.

Kharakhorin, in Uvurkhangai aimag. Today there are five smaller hydroelectric power stations in Kharkhorin, Chigjiin, Bogdyn, Mankhan and Guulin. Several larger plants are planned. Although water is relatively scarce in southern and eastern parts, Mongolia's numerous fast-flowing rivers makes the development of hydro-electric power an ideal solution to the energy problems the country faces.

RENEWABLE ENERGY

Geographically, Mongolia is located in the Central Asian plateau. This means that the country enjoys a large number of clear, sunny days – between 2,700 and 3,200 hours of sunshine annually. High winds also sweep the country at speeds of between four and nine metres per second. This offers great potential for harnessing solar and wind power to generate electric-ity and such renewable resources may prove invaluable to the Mongolian energy industry in the future.

THE ENVIRONMENT

In recent years, Mongolia's ecosystem has changed significantly. The country has suffered from soil erosion and desertification, leading to an increase in violent sand storms. Water supplies have declined. Increasing numbers of plant and animal species have found their way on to the endangered list. With help from other nations, the government is attempting to address these environmental issues and is making plans to halt or reverse the damage. The country's severe, dry climate can make this difficult, but programmes to plant more trees can prevent further desertification, for example, and ensure that vital habitats are preserved.

AIR POLLUTION

Air pollution has become one of the biggest environmental issues in the twenty-first century, particularly in Ulaanbaatar. This is caused by vehicle fumes, gases released through industry, including power plants, and fumes from the coal burned in the *gher* districts in the north, east and west of the capital. Around 130,000 families live in these districts and they burn 500,000 to 600,000 tonnes of coal a year.

Pollution caused by vehicles is rising as car ownership in the cities increases. More than 100,000 cars and other vehicles are now used in the capital. Most of them are second-hand – people cannot afford to buy new cars – and so are far more environmentally damaging.

A person living in Ulaanbaatar inhales 200kg of smoke every year. This pollution is already having an adverse effect on the population, demonstrated by increased numbers of cases of cancer and respiratory disease.

WASTE MANAGEMENT

Waste is also an increasing problem in Ulaanbaatar. There are no waste-processing plants, so incineration is the only way of disposing of most waste. There are no major recycling programmes in operation, although some glass and plastic containers are collected and reused by individuals.

Despite the current situation, some plans are underway to improve waste-management in Mongolia. A Japanese aid agency, JICA, began a programme in 2007 in which waste containers were constructed near apartment buildings. At scheduled times, usually three or four times a week, trucks collect the waste. When this programme began, there were concerns that the waste containers might spread disease in the overcrowded city. It was suggested that people may search the containers looking for waste they could use, which would be a health risk. However, the benefits of such waste collection are seen to outweigh the drawbacks.

Air pollution increases during the winter as inhabitants of the *gher* districts burn coal.

Water pollution is caused by the location of an industrial district in the Tuul river basin.

Problems with Water Supply

Mongolia's rivers are the main source of freshwater to supply the needs of the population, so the rise in river pollution in recent years has caused concern. Factors that have contributed to the pollution include natural disasters and human activity. The River Tuul, an important freshwater supply for Ulaanbaatar, has experienced a decrease in volume and some years ago parts of it ran dry. Another river, the Selbe, once flowed through the capital, but this ran dry in the 1990s.

Water pollution does not only occur in the cities, however: mining activities in rural areas are also responsible. There was once a famous waterfall called Ulaan Tsutgalan in Uvurkhangai aimag, but this disappeared after its source river was artificially blocked and dammed, and its water polluted by gold mining.

Farmland Damage

In Mongolia around 115,000 hectares of land is used for agriculture. Although 110,000 hectares of this is used for grazing, a recent study showed that 80 per cent of this land is already suffering from erosion. This is a major problem for those Mongolians who still follow nomadic farming traditions. If they cannot find good land on which to graze and raise their herds, this ancient way of life may one day die out completely.

Forestry

Only five per cent of Mongolia is now covered with forest. Huvsgul's taiga and the Khentii mountain range were once covered in forest. The Tujiin nars (pine) forest in Selenge aimag, on the border with Russia, has suffered one of the most dramatic cases of deforestation in the region. Situated at the southern tip of Siberia, this was once a beautiful tree-covered area, until illegal logging stripped it bare and drove out all the wildlife.

In the early 2000s, a programme of reforestation began as a result of mass publicity about the region. Different organisations and groups now contribute to the programme by planting a certain amount of trees to help build up forest cover in Tujiin.

As of 2005, Ulaanbaatar had around 247,000 head of livestock.

Mongolia first established a capital city around 370 years ago. Since this time, the name and location of the capital have changed several times. The current name, Ulaanbaatar, was adopted in 1924, and the city is now located in north-central Mongolia.

URBAN LIFE

Today, approximately 60 per cent of Mongolia's population lives in urban areas and this number increases by about one per cent every year. In 2006, the population of Ulaanbaatar was estimated to be around 965,300 and it is now thought to be over one million. This rise has taken place in part because rural families are increasingly electing to send their children to school and university, and must move to the cities – particularly Ulaanbaatar – to do so.

As migration to the capital increases, issues of urban infrastructure have become a key challenge. Most of the migrants cannot affort apartment buildings, so they settle in the *gher* districts on the outskirts of the city.

In the 1970s this was one of the tallest buildings in Ulaanbaatar.

MONGOLIAN CITIES

Most of Mongolia's cities were established or increased in size during the socialist era, and were built with Russian assistance. There are three main cities in Mongolia. The largest is Ulaanbaatar, followed by Darkhan and then Erdenet. The centre of Selenge aimag was once the city of Sukhbaatar, but its status was later replaced by that of a *soum*, or district.

The northernmost city, Darkhan, is located on one of the major railway intersections and has a population of around 87,000. Erdenet, to the south of it, has 80,000 inhabitants. The population of Sukhbaatar *soum* is estimated at around 30,000.

Cities are often made up of apartments in the centre, with *gher* districts on the outskirts.

US president George W. Bush on a visit to Mongolia in 2005.

International relations are now very important to the Mongolians. While they aim to maintain the relationships with their neighbours China and Russia, building new relationships with democracies such as the United States is considered equally important.

THE UNITED STATES

Mongolia has enjoyed diplomatic relations with the United States for more than 20 years. Prior to the introduction of democracy, many western countries – and the United States in particular – were largely thought of as imperialist powers by the regime in Mongolia. Since the democratic revolution, however, relations between the two countries have improved and many young Mongolians choose to study or work in the United States. The heads of state have made official visits and have planned collaborations in a number of areas.

In 2005 US president George W. Bush visited Mongolia. He and the Mongolian president committed to developing a working partnership to further improve relations. In the aftermath of the terror-

Soldiers on a training exercise. Mongolia has both an army and air force.

ist attack on New York on 11 September 2001, Mongolia expressed its support for the United States' War on Terror, and has joined other nations in fighting this. These and other joint activities demonstrate the increasing trust and working relationship between the two countries.

CHINA AND RUSSIA

Mongolia's location, with borders on both China and Russia, has resulted in a long association with these two nations. In the socialist era Russia exerted a strong influence over Mongolian political decisions and ways of life. Since the market reform, however, Mongolia has also improved its relationship with China, one of the most rapidly developing nations in the world. The Chinese influence can now be seen in parts of Mongolia.

PEACEKEEPING OPERATIONS

Although Mongolia is currently not involved in any international disputes, Mongolian armed forces have had a presence in a number of peacekeeping activities, including those in Iran and Kosovo. The country has an army and air force, but, being landlocked, it has no navy.

ASIA

Mongolia's location in northeast Asia means its land and infrastructure will be of increasing importance in matters such as exporting the resources being tapped in Siberia. The easternmost aimag, Dornod, will be particularly significant, as it borders both Russia and China. Choibalsan aimag already has a rail link to Russia, but in order to connect to China, a further 400km of railway will need to be built. The workload taken on by Manuul railway station, connecting China and Russia, has increased in the past few years and a railroad to Choibalsan will be established. This offers the region an opportunity to improve its economy, as facilities will be needed to service the railroad during building and after it becomes operational.

This aimag was the site of the Khalkh river battles in 1939 and boasts a beautiful natural landscape that includes Lake Buir and the Hangayn mountain range. Such attractions will draw increasing numbers of visitors. This is also true of other parts of Mongolia, and improved transport links to countries such as Russia and China will benefit the country as a whole.

Aimag The largest administrative unit in Mongolia. There are 21 aimags, which are divided into *soums*, or districts.

Arid A term used to describe an environment that generally receives less than 250mm annual rainfall.

Airag A traditional Mongolian drink made from fermented horse's milk.

Argal (mouflon) A species of wild sheep with a pair of curved horns.

Bayan khodood The title given to the last horse in the two-year-old race during the festival of Naadam.

Birth rate The number of children born in a year per 1,000 of the population.

Bituun 'To close down' – the name given to the eve of Tsagaan sar, New Year.

Buuz A type of steamed dumpling stuffed with minced meat (usually mutton or beef). *Buuz* is mostly served during Tsagaan sar.

Desertification The spread of desert into land that was previously used for farming or habitation.

Ecosystem A system that represents the relationships within a community of living things (plants or animals) and between the community and its non-living environment. An ecosystem can be as small as a pond or as large as the Earth.

European Union A group of countries that have joined together to achieve closer political, social, economic and environmental cooperation.

GDP (Gross Domestic Product) The monetary value of goods and services produced by a country in a single year.

Gher A round makeshift dwelling, easily constructed and dismantled into component parts. *Gher* districts are often found on the outskirts of cities.

Gobi A large desert area in the south of Mongolia, with a hot climate and low levels of rainfall.

Hydroelectricity Electricity generated by water as it passes through turbines.

Ibex A species of wild goat with large horns, found in mountainous areas.

Idee A type of layered confection made during Tsagaan sar and Naadam, built up from an odd number of layers of biscuit.

Infrastructure The transport, communication and services (water, electricity, sewerage etc.) networks and systems that support an economy and society.

Khadag A scarf-shaped strip, highly honoured in Buddhism, finely woven from high-quality silk.

Malazai A rare species of bear found only in the Gobi Desert.

Moriton A horse-mounted warrior of ancient times.

Naadam The national holiday celebrating Mongolian independence, held annually in July. The festival comprises a series of competitive events in wrestling, horse-racing and archery.

Nomad A person who moves around rather than settling in one place. In Mongolia the traditional lifestyle was nomadic as herders moved around to find the best pasture to raise their livestock.

Plateau A relatively flat-topped upland area.

Semi-arid A term used to describe an environment that generally receives 250–400mm annual rainfall.

Socialism A social system in which everything is owned by the state, and private property is forbidden. Socialism is largely associated with Communism and was the regime in Mongolia during its period of rule by the Soviet Union.

Soum A district within an aimag.

Steppe A treeless, semi-arid area of land characterised by grassy plains.

Takhi A rare wild horse, once on the verge of extinction in Mongolia, but recently successfully reintroduced.

Tsaagan sar 'White Moon'. The lunar New Year, celebrated in the East.

Tuiren A type of devastating sandstorm that occurs in the in Gobi Desert. These can spread for hundreds of kilometres.

Zolgolt A traditional Mongolian greeting, usually given at New Year, in which young people hold older family members under the elbows to indicate their support.

FURTHER INFORMATION

BOOKS TO READ:
Facts About Mongolia by Da. Ganbold (Admon, 2000)
A guide for travellers of all ages.

Mongolia Tourist Guide by Yuri Kruchkin and M. Enkhbayar (Ulaanbaatar, 2003). Tourist guide.

Chinggis Khaan's Mongolia by S. Uranbileg and E. Amarbileg (Ulaanbaatar, 2006). All about Mongolia for travellers.

WEBSITES:
CIA World Factbook
https://www.cia.gov/library/publications/the-world-factbook/geos/mg.html
The US Central Intelligence Agency's online factbook, containing statistics about all areas of the country, including population, economy and government.

Wikipedia
http://en.wikipedia.org/wiki/Mongolia
A free online encyclopedia, with facts and statistics about Mongolia, its history, people and culture

DEVELOPMENT INFORMATION:
United Nations Development Programme (UNDP)
www.undp.mn/new

TOURIST INFORMATION:
Discover Mongolia
www.mongoliatourism.gov.mn
The Mongolian government's official tourism website.

Numbers shown in **bold** refer to pages with maps, graphic illustrations or photographs.